Healthy Weight Loss Smoothies: To Lose Weight, Live Long and Detox

NATALIA ZORINA

ISBN: 9781522018452

CONTENTS

Who am I?

My name is Natalia Zorina. I am a wife, mother, certified nutritionist, personal trainer, online coach, fitness blogger with over 100K audience, fitness bikini Canada national level athlete, and fitness mobile application founder.

In my first book "30 Days Fit Body Meal And Workout Plan: Become Your Own Personal Trainer, Your Best Home Workout Guide" I've opened up all basics necessary to build a body of your dream and become healthier. A book you got in your hands is devoted to a magic tool called "smoothies". I personally practice integrating smoothies into a diet of my own and my clients, because they are amazing micro nutrients source and help to lose weight, detoxify, fight disease, and live long.

Introduction

Most of the people blend bananas with milk, strawberries and protein powder when they want to have a smoothie. Need more smoothies ideas? Then you got the right book. Congratulations! You got a source of ideas for smoothies, which you can easily implement just every single day. In most of the recipes, we did not provide "directions" or "cooking method" simply because all smoothies do not require cooking at all. All you need to do is just to blend all ingredients in a food processor until smooth and creamy. And one more thing you should be doing after that is to ENJOY.

Smoothies are very helpful when you need to replace a meal or to add colors to your diet because they need no cooking and don't take any of your time. You can make one in few minutes and be worry free until the next meal.

Where to find unusual ingredients? You will see lots of unusual ingredients in this book. Such as pomegranate powder or apple rose water. You never see them on the shelf of the regular grocery store. But, do not worry! They exist (smiling), reasonably priced and very good for your health. I advise getting those ingredients online, from a very popular website: www.iherb.com and claim your 5% DISCOUNT using a promo code FLS735 or follow the link https://iherb.com/?rcode=FLS735. Please pay attention, that this benefit works both for NEW and EXISTING customers.

Benefits of smoothies

In general words, smoothies help you to lose weight, detoxify, fight disease, and live long. But let me give you some more details.

Smoothies are incredibly delicious and soft. You can drink them with a large straw or eat with a regular spoon. Correctly prepared smoothies undoubtedly belong to healthy food. Smoothie is perfect for dinner. You can replace dinner with smoothies. The use of smoothies instead of dinner will help get rid of extra pounds.

Benefits of drinking smoothies:

- Smoothies preserves all the vitamins that make up the ingredients of smoothies. You can combine smoothies with fresh juices, fruits, and vegetables.

- Smoothies give a lot of energy because it contains a lot of vitamins and antioxidants.

- Due to the presence of fibers in smoothies, smoothies do not create a heaviness in the stomach.

- The use of smoothies allows you to remove toxins from your body.

- Smoothies are used to maintain vitality, to reduce excess weight.

- Smoothies can be attributed to "anti-stress" foods.

- They contain a large number of vitamins, micro-elements strengthen our immunity.

Recipes

#1. JUICY MANGO & BANANA MIX

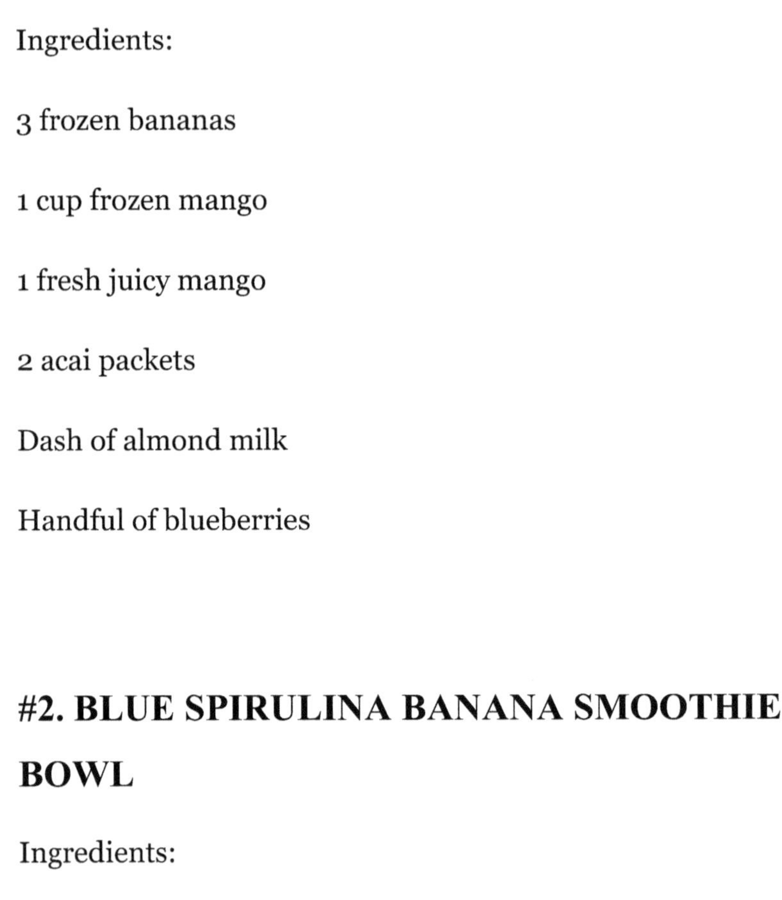

Ingredients:

3 frozen bananas

1 cup frozen mango

1 fresh juicy mango

2 acai packets

Dash of almond milk

Handful of blueberries

#2. BLUE SPIRULINA BANANA SMOOTHIE BOWL

Ingredients:

3 frozen bananas

1 tsp blue spirulina powder

50-100 ml coconut milk

#3. CACAO SMOOTHIE BOWL

Ingredients:

1,5 cup Almond milk

2 soft bananas

1/2 Avocado

1,5 tbsp raw cacao powder

1/4 cup Peanut butter or Almond butter

Drizzle of pure maple syrup

#4. TWO BOWLS: PINK AND YELLOW

Ingredients for the yellow blend:

Frozen banana

frozen mango

turmeric

coconut milk

Ingredients for the pink blend:

Frozen banana

frozen pitaya

almond milk

coco water

#5. STRAWBERRY SMOOTHIE BOWL

Ingredients:

banana

Strawberry

Topping:

coconut chips

cacao nib

#6. BANANA HAZELNUT COCONUT MILKSHAKE

Ingredients:

1 frozen banana

3 tbsp oats

1 tbsp ground hazelnuts

1 tsp maca powder (optional)

1 tsp cacao nibs

200 ml coconut milk

1/5 Tsp vanilla bean powder

A pinch of salt

#7. BLACKBERRY SMOOTHIE

Ingredients:

blackberry

banana

Chocolate sauce:

1 tsp cacao powder

1 tsp liquid coconut oil

1/2 tsp maple syrup

#8. MANGO PUDDING

Ingredients:

350g frozen cauliflower

1/2 mango

1/2 Tsp cardamom

1/4 tsp turmeric

50g coconut cream

1.5 tsp psyllium husks

50g date paste

A dash of water or plant milk

Optional:

additional sweetener of your choice

Directions:

Cook or steam cauliflower until soft. Add all ingredients to a high-speed blender and blend until smooth. Transfer to a bowl and enjoy warm with toppings of your choice.

#9. AVOCADO CHOCOLATE PUDDING

Ingredients:

1 avocado

2 bananas

150-200 ml water (it depends on how you like the consistency)

20g cocoa powder

Optional: 15g chocolate protein powder

#10. AQUA GREEN GRAPE SMOOTHIE BOWL

Ingredients:

blended 1/4 cup of chilled young coconut

2 frozen bananas

a handful of frozen grapes

1 Tbsp coconut cream

pinch of blue spirulina

Topping:

frozen grapes

dried coconut cubes

dragon fruit

#11. CHOCOLATE CHIA PUDDING

Ingredients:

2 frozen medium size banana

1 scoop of protein powder

1 tbsp of whole coconut milk

For the chia pudding:

3/4 cup of coconut milk

3 Tbsp. of chia seeds

1/4 drop of vanilla extract

Directions:

Mix all the chia pudding ingredients together and pop it into the fridge for 5 minutes. Take out and mix again. Repeat this 2 times every 5 minutes, so that the chia seeds expand properly. Pop it back into the fridge for at least 2 hours to become nice and thick. For best results: leave it overnight.

How to assemble your chia cup:

1. Blend all the chocolate base ingredients in a high-speed blender.

2. Using a spoon gently fill up your cup with the chocolate base.

3. Then using another spoon gently place the chia pudding on top.

4. Top with frozen blueberries.

5. Garnish with edible flowers.

#12. RASPBERRY CASHEW MORNING PUDDING

Ingredients:

2 cups Cashew nuts, soaked overnight

2 cups Frozen raspberries

1 cup Coconut milk

#13. AÇAI NICE CREAM HEAVEN

Ingredients:

1 frozen banana

2 frozen mango

1 cup açai

a handful of blueberries

1.5 cups soy milk.

Topping:

chocolate

peanut Butter

cacao Snack balls

sprinkles

#14. GREEN SMOOTHIE

Ingredients:

2 bananas

1 mango

1 avocado

1 bunch of kale

moringa powder

#15. CHERRY CHOCOLATE & CHIA SMOOTHIE PARFAIT

Ingredients:

2 tbsp chia

1 tbsp gluten-free oats

1/2 cup (120ml) almond milk

8-10 fresh cherries

2 tbsp dark chocolate chips

1/2 banana, frozen and chopped

1/3 cup frozen mixed berries (cherry, raspberry, blackberry, and blueberry)

1 scoop (20g) plant-based vanilla protein powder

1 tbsp hemp seeds

Directions:

1. Combine chia, oats and almond milk in a bowl. Stir, then wait 10

minutes and stir again to stop clumps from forming. Place in fridge to absorb overnight, or at least for one hour.

2. When ready remove chia from the fridge and stir to remove any formed clumps. Add more almond milk if desired for preferred pudding consistency.

3. Cut cherries in half and remove the pits. Place cherries halves around the inside of a glass jar (alternatively you can use a bowl), then fill with chia pudding. Top pudding with a layer of dark chocolate chips and place to the side.

4. Add frozen banana, frozen berries, protein powder, and hemp seeds to your blender. Add a splash of almond milk for blending. (The amount of almond milk required will depend on how powerful your blender is. I used about 1/4 cup (60 ml)). Blend ingredients until smooth.

5. Top chia pudding with frozen smoothie blend. Sprinkle with star sprinkles and serve with a cherry on top.

#16. RED GRAPE SMOOTHIE BOWL

Ingredients:

Base:

2 frozen bananas

a handful of red grapes

1 Tbsp coconut cream

2 Tbsp of pomegranate powder

Topping:

frosty jumbo red grapes

coconut cubes

dragon fruit balls

#17. MANGO TURMERIC PROTEIN SMOOTHIE BOWL

Ingredients:

1 cup of frozen mango

1 frozen banana

1/3 cup of coconut milk

1/2 teaspoon of turmeric

1 scoop of vegan vanilla protein powder

Topping:

blueberries

raspberries

protein clusters

a dash of turmeric

#18. RADISH & GINGER ANTIOXIDANT SMOOTHIE BOWL

Ingredients:

4 small radishes

1 cup frozen mixed berries

½ cup frozen mango

½ a banana

½ cup cold pressed apple juice

½ cup water

½ teaspoon of ground ginger

Decorate with swirls of coconut yogurt and slices of fresh ginger and radish for some crunch.

#19. SIMPLE STRAWBERRY SMOOTHIE BOWL

Ingredients:

1 cup frozen strawberries

3 frozen bananas

1/8 cup of coconut milk

#20. THE PERFECT MANGO STRAWBERRY SMOOTHIE

Ingredients:

Mango smoothie layer:

2 mangoes, diced

3/4 cup plain lowfat Greek yogurt

1/2 teaspoon fresh minced ginger

1/2 cup coconut water

Ice

Strawberry smoothie layer:

1 1/2 cups chopped strawberries

1 banana

3/4 cup plain lowfat Greek yogurt

1/2 teaspoon fresh minced ginger

1/2 cup coconut water

Ice

#21. CLASSIC GREEN MONSTER SMOOTHIES

Ingredients:

1 cup almond/soy/rice milk

1 cup steamed kale leaves or baby spinach leaves

1 large ripe frozen banana (chopped)

1 Tbsp almond butter or peanut butter

1 Tbsp chia seeds or ground flaxseed

Pinch of ground cinnamon

1 scoop of protein powder (vanilla taste for example)

Ice

#22. PINK PANTHER BOWL

Ingredients:

2 cups frozen banana (chopped)

1 cup of frozen raspberries

1 heaping Tbsp. of pomegranate powder

2 Tbsp. Apple Rose Water

#23. FRESH MANGO SMOOTHIE

Ingredients:

3 frozen banana

1 frozen mango

1 fresh juicy mango

1 / 2 cups of almond milk

1 cup of blueberries

#24. DOUBLE LAYER SMOOTHIE

Ingredients:

Yellow layer:

2 cups of frozen mango

1 bananas

1 orange

Pink Layer:

1 cup frozen cherries

1 banana

1 / 4 cups of Pitaya

#25. MERRY BERRY

Ingredients:

1 glass of frozen strawberries

3/4 cup frozen raspberries

1/2 cup frozen blueberries

2 kiwis

1 glass of orange juice

#26. VEGAN CHOCOLATE SMOOTHIE

Ingredients:

2 bananas

6 ice cubes

1 tbsp coconut oil

1 tbsp dairy free plain yogurt

1 tbsp chia seeds

2 tbsp hemp seeds

1 tsp camu camu powder

1 tbsp raw cacao powder

¼ cup coconut milk (or unsweetened almond milk)

#27. GREEN PINEAPPLE SMOOTHIE

Ingredients:

1 vanilla yogurt

1 banana

1 cup pineapple

1 bunch of fresh spinach

1/2 cup of apple juice

Ice (optional)

#28. LIGHT SUMMER SMOOTHIE BOWL

Ingredients:

20 strawberries

400 grams of sliced pineapple

200 ml of coconut milk

Toppings:

Raspberries

Strawberries

Sliced Almonds

#29. BLUEBERRY KIWI PROTEIN SMOOTHIE

Ingredients:

½ cup blueberries (fresh or frozen)

2 kiwis

2 mint leaves

3 tbsp hemp seeds

4 ice cubes

¼ cup vanilla almond milk (or unsweetened)

#30. PINEAPPLE AVOCADO SMOOTHIE

Ingredients:

2 cups pineapple

1 mango

1 ripe avocado

Juice from 1 lemon

1 tbsp chia seeds

¼ cup coconut milk

#31. HONEYDEW SMOOTHIE BOWL

Ingredients:

½ of 1 honeydew

2 tbsp shredded coconut

2 tbsp hemp seeds

2 cups kale, stems removed

¼ cup old fashioned oats

¼ cup coconut milk

#32. CINNAMON CHOCOLATE PROTEIN SMOOTHIE

Ingredients:

1/3 cup oats

1/2 teaspoon cinnamon

1/2 container greek yogurt

1/3 scoop Cinnamon protein powder

2 tablespoon cocoa powder

1/3 cup almond milk

1/2 of a frozen banana

5 ice cubes

#33. COCONUT AND BERRIES BOWL

Ingredients:

1 1/2 Cups Frozen Mixed Berries

1/2 Cup Oats

1/4 Cup Coconut Shavings

1 Tbsp Honey/Agave Nectar

1 Cup Almond Milk

Topping:

Chia Seeds

Berries

Coconut Shavings

Nuts

Instructions

#34. PEAR AND MANGO SMOOTHIE

Ingredients:

1 cup almond milk

1 mango

1 pear

1 glass of blueberries

1 serving of soy protein powder

Ice cubes to taste

#35. RASPBERRY PEACH SMOOTHIE

Ingredients:

1 cup frozen raspberries

¾ cup chopped fresh peaches

¼ cup vanilla Greek yogurt

⅓ cup vanilla almond milk

#36. PEANUT BUTTER BANANA CHOCOLATE SMOOTHIE

Ingredients:

1 tbsp RAW cocoa powder

2 frozen Bananas

1 tbsp almond Butter

1 cup Almond/Soy/Rice milk

#37. SUPER DETOX SMOOTHIE

Ingredients:

1.5 cups of cabbage leaf (or spinach)

1/2 cucumber

2 stalks of celery

1 small lemon without a peel

1 ripe banana

1 cup pineapple

2 tbsp chia seeds

1 teaspoon of spirulina powder

1 cup almond milk

1 glass of water

Ice

#38. EXTREME CHOCOLATE BANANA SMOOTHIE

Ingredients:

3 frozen bananas

¾ cup almond/soy/rice milk

¼ cup almond butter

2 tbsp unsweetened raw cocoa powder

2 tbsp honey

2 tbsp raw coconut oil

#39. MANGO KIWI BOWL

Ingredients:

2 frozen bananas

2 cups frozen mango

2 tbsp chia seeds

1,5 cups almond/soy/rice milk

2 fresh kiwis

Toppings:

2 tablespoons chia seeds

chopped nuts

coconut

other fruits and seeds

#40. TRIPLE BERRY SMOOTHIE

Ingredients:

2 frozen bananas

1 cup frozen strawberries

1 cup almond/soy/rice milk

1 cup frozen blueberries

1 cup frozen raspberries

#41. VANILLA SMOOTHIE

Ingredients:

3 frozen ripe banana

1/2 ripe avocado

1/4 cup almond milk

1 serving of vanilla vegan protein powder

1/2 teaspoon spirulina powder

Toppings:

Chia seeds

Grated coconut

Fresh fruit (berries, kiwi, mango, banana)

Granola

#42. IMMUNE BOOSTING SMOOTHIE

Ingredients:

1 large handful Spinach

1 thumb sized Piece of Ginger

2 Medjool Dates

2 Oranges (juiced)

1/2 Lemon (juiced)

1/4 tsp Turmeric Powder

#43. GREEN BERRY SMOOTHIE

Ingredients:

Berries layer:

1-1/2 cups halved strawberries

1 banana

1/2- cup plain nonfat yogurt

2 tablespoons honey

1 cup crushed ice

Green layer:

2 cups torn kale leaves, packed

1 green apple, quartered (skin-on)

1 banana

1/2- cup plain nonfat yogurt

1/4- cup skim milk

2 tbsp honey

1 cup crushed ice

Directions:

Combine strawberries and banana slices in a bowl and place in the freezer for 20 minutes. In a blender, combine kale, apple slices, banana, yogurt, honey and crushed ice; blend until creamy and smooth. Divide mixture between FOUR 8-ounce glasses; place in the freezer for 20 minutes.Rinse blender; combine strawberries, banana, yogurt, honey, and ice; blend until creamy and smooth. Remove prepared smoothies from the freezer. Pour the strawberry mixture over the kale mixture. Serve immediately.

#44. SMOOTH BANANA BOWL

Ingredients:

230 ml soy/rice/almond milk

1 frozen banana

200 ml of natural yogurt

1 serving of protein powder (vanilla taste for example)

5 vanilla biscuits

Cinnamon (optional)

Ice

#45. PINK POMEGRANATE SMOOTHIE

Ingredients:

1/2 cup natural, no flavor yogurt

2 soft fresh bananas

1/2 cup pomegranate juice

1/4 cup honey

1 cup of ice

Topping:

3 tablespoons pomegranate seeds

#46. DETOX SPINACH SMOOTHIE

Ingredients:

1 cup spinach (chopped)

1 cup soy/rice/almond milk

1 glass of fresh pineapple (chopped)

1 banana (chopped)

1 tbsp chia seeds

#47. SUPER BRIGHT SMOOTHIE BOWL

Ingredients:

½ cup rice/soy/almond milk

1 glass of frozen or fresh berries (any kind)

½ raw beets of medium size (chopped)

1 banana (chopped)

¼ cup flax seed

2 bunches spinach or lettuce leaves

#48. PECAN BERRY CUP

Ingredients:

5 strawberries

1 frozen banana

1 tablespoon pecan

2 dates

1 tablespoon oats

200 ml rice/almond/soy milk

1 cup blackberries

Directions:

Place all the ingredients (except blackberry) in the blender and mix them until smooth. Blend blackberry separately and then put everything in one cup. Add the strawberry puree and enjoy.

#49. GREEN AND YELLOW MANGO MATCHA SMOOTHIE

Ingredients:

1 Frozen Ripe Banana

1 Handful Spinach

1 tbsp Oats

1/2 tbsp Matcha Powder

1 cup soy/almond or rice milk

1/2 fresh Mango

#50. PRETTY CHERRY AND SWEET PEACH SMOOTHIE

Ingredients:

6 oz Black Cherry OR Peach Chobani Greek Yogurt

1 cup pitted fresh or frozen sweet cherries

1 fresh peach, sliced OR 1 cup frozen peach slices

1 - 2 cups fresh or flash-frozen baby spinach

1/4 - 1/2 cup milk

#51. BROWN CINNAMON CHIA PUDDING PARFAIT

Ingredients:

Cinnamon Rawnola:

8-10 Medjool Dates

1/2 cup (45g) Rolled Oats

1 tsp Ground Cinnamon

Chia Pudding:

1 cup (240ml) Plant Milk of your choice

1 tsp Agave Nectar or another sweetener

3 tbsp Chia Seeds

Berry Smoothie:

1 Frozen Banana

1/2 cup Frozen Berries

1 cup Plant Milk of your choice

1 tsp Agave Nectar optional

Directions:

Make the chia pudding the night before you want to serve the parfait, or at least two hours before. Mix all the chia pudding ingredients together in a bowl then cover and refrigerate, stirring after an hour, then after two hours. After that, you can leave the pudding covered in the fridge for 2-3 days.

To make the rawnola, pit the dates. If they are a little dry, soak them in some just boiled water for 15 minutes, then drain before adding to a blender with the cinnamon and oats. Blend until the mixture comes together in chunks.

Blend the smoothie ingredients until smooth. Depending on how thick your smoothie is, you can add extra plant milk to thin it out a bit if you desire. Layer everything in a glass and enjoy!

www.ingramcontent.com/pod-product-compliance
Lightning Source LLC
LaVergne TN
LVHW011052030225
802831LV00008B/327

* 9 7 8 1 5 2 2 0 1 8 4 5 2 *